The Everyday Email Eradication Plan:

How to Get Your Inbox down to Zero and Keep it that way in 6 Easy Steps!

Introduction

I want to thank you and congratulate you for downloading the book, *"The Everyday Email Eradication Plan: How to Get Your Email Inbox down to Zero and Keep it that way in 6 Easy Steps!"*.

This book contains proven steps and strategies on

how to tame the beast that is your email inbox. We all know that an untamed email inbox can prevent any productivity from happening and destroy your office efficiency. An email inbox that is not under control is a time bomb just waiting to go off in your face.

This book is also part of the *Technology Dominance* series that I've been cooking up in my cubicle. I'm going to take my techie knowledge and make it available to you, the reader! Stay tuned for future installments in the *Technology Dominance* series so that you can be the new Genius on the block!

Thanks again for downloading this book, I hope you enjoy it!

This document is geared towards providing exact and reliable information in regards to the topic and issue covered. The publication is sold with the idea that the publisher is not required to render accounting, officially permitted, or otherwise, qualified services. If advice is necessary, legal or professional, a practiced individual in the profession should be ordered.

- From a Declaration of Principles which was accepted and approved equally by a Committee of the American Bar Association and a

publisher. All rights reserved.

The information provided herein is stated to be truthful and consistent, in that any liability, in terms of inattention or otherwise, by any usage or abuse of any policies, processes, or directions contained within is the solitary and utter responsibility of the recipient reader. Under

purposes solely, and is universal as so. The presentation of the information is without contract or any type of guarantee assurance.

The trademarks that are used are without any consent, and the publication of the trademark is without permission or backing by the trademark owner. All trademarks and brands

1: Away with the unwanted

The first step is probably the easiest for most. If you don't want to keep something then delete it. Get it out of your life by taking it out of your email inbox forever.

Be familiar with how to do this on your smartphone or computer. It's better to do this right away when you see the message. Don't let it hang out for a long period of time. That's how your inbox became full to begin with, right?

2: Head them off at the pass

We all know that there are emails we keep getting week after week after week. Usually these people get our email addresses from when we sign up for contests or things such as that.

But did you know that at the bottom of these email

there is almost always a "unsubscribe from mailing list" button to click. Doesn't it make sense to stop these annoyances at the source instead of deleting over and over again every single week?

3: Good Habits are ok.

We all have good habits that we do every single day. Brushing our teeth. Combing our hair. But did you know there need to be good tech habits as well?

Create a reminder to clean out your inbox daily or weekly, that's up to you. I recommend daily since we all get some many emails every single day.

After a few weeks you'll find that this good habit will also become second nature to you and you'll be on top of your email in no time!

4: Work smarter not harder.

A little known tip is that email programs will have a built in search bar that you can use to gain even further control of your inbox.

Use the search field to bring up multiples of the same email you are wanting to delete. Then select them all at once and hit that delete button to destroy them.Most email programs will also allow you to mark the sender or email as "junk" which you can then have your email delete from here on out.

5: The computer works for you.

What if there was a way to have your computer do most of the deleting and sorting for you. I'm happy to say that you can do this in most email programs and it makes all the difference in the world.

Create what is called a "s m a r t   r u l e"   t o

automatically file or delete certain email messages. It will cut minutes out of your day which added up over the course of a year could equal up to multiple saved hours!

6: Everything has a place.

Getting your inbox to zero does not necessarily mean deleting everything. We rather want to have control over everything and know where it is. It's when you have everything in it's place and you don't have 1,000s of unsorted emails that you will then have complete control of your email inbox.

Create folders that you can use to sort out the emails like if your email program was a big filing cabinet. You don't want to have any travel themed emails in a folder that's for email regarding pet info so be wary for what email you're putting in what folder.

Conclusion

Thank you again for downloading this book!

I hope this book was able to help you to finally gain control of your email inbox and see the light at the end of the tunnel.

The next step is to keep at it every week so that you can continue to see a sparkly clean and useful mailbox..

Finally, if you enjoyed this book, then I'd like to ask you for a favor, would you be kind enough to leave a review for this book on Amazon? It'd be greatly appreciated!

Thank you and good luck!